Guide to Arrive, Survive and Thrive in Rio de Janeiro

Norman Ratcliffe

Clink Street

London | New York

Published by Clink Street Publishing 2015

Copyright © 2015

First edition.

ISBN: 978-1-911110-00-2
E-Book: 978-1-911110-01-9

Guide to Arrive, Survive and Thrive in Rio de Janeiro: Tips for Staying Safe and Healthy

Essential Health and Survival Facts Seen Through the Eyes of a Long-term Visitor from the UK

*

Professor Norman Ratcliffe

Acknowledgements

I would like to thank my Brasilian colleagues and students in the Universidade Federal Fluminense, Instituto de Biologia, for their wonderful friendship, enthusiasm and help during my stay in Rio. I would particularly like to mention Professors Cicero Brasileiro, Dilvani Santos and Helena Castro for their support, sense of humour and optimism throughout.

"Brazil is not Europe or the USA and can seem like a foreign planet to the visitor, so be prepared!"

Traveller's Guide to Rio de Janeiro

You have been saving up for your tickets and accommodation, time is flying by and, before you know it, you have to commit yourself to going to Rio de Janeiro for the Carnival, New Year or Rock in Rio events. However, the news of the demonstrations in Brazil is increasingly worrying regarding health and safety issues in the country. Look at the unrest in Egypt, Libya and Turkey and it is natural to ask whether Brazil is the next country destined for major disruptions and anarchy.

I have written this guide as I have been a frequent visitor to Rio de Janeiro for over 20 years and so am in an excellently well qualified position to reveal the highs and lows of this marvellous city and introduce the reader to the fantastic country of Brazil. In the next few years, millions of visitors will arrive in Rio to attend Carnival, New Year and Rock in Rio celebrations and will need constructive advice on how to avoid the possible pitfalls of such a trip. This book presents tips on survival and health matters in Rio de Janeiro, but many of these are also applicable to other cities throughout Brazil. A great number of these tips will not be given in most guidebooks to Brazil as many of these will have been written by tour companies or armchair travellors and not by somebody actually living in Rio.

Norman Ratcliffe recently 'retired' after spending 25 years as a biomedical research professor at Swansea University. He has been a Visiting Professor at the Fiocruz Research Institute and Federal University Fluminense Rio de Janeiro for the last 20 years. He has published over 200 books and research papers on immunology, cancer invasion, influenza, tropical diseases and MRSA, and is the author of *It's Your Life: End the Confusion from Inconsistent Health Advice.*

https://www.amazon.co.uk/Norman-Ratcliffe/e/B004HCA9NU

Contents

Introduction

Thinking about travelling to Rio for the Carnival, New Year or Rock in Rio?

You have been saving up for your tickets and accommodation, time is flying by and, before you know it, you have to commit yourself to going to Rio de Janeiro for the Carnival, New Year or Rock in Rio. However, the news of the demonstrations in Brazil is increasingly worrying regarding health and safety issues in that country. Look at the unrest in Egypt, Libya and Turkey and it is natural to ask whether Brazil is the next country destined for major disruptions and anarchy.

I have written this guide as I have been a frequent visitor to Rio de Janeiro for over 20 years and lived there for the last 3 years. I am therefore in an excellently well qualified position to reveal the highs and lows of this marvellous city as well as to introduce the reader to the fantastic country of Brazil.

Millions of visitors attended the World Cup and Olympics and arrive in Rio each year for the Carnival, New Year celebrations and vacations. They will need constructive advice on how to avoid the possible pitfalls of such a trip.

Recent visitors to Rio from overseas have already expressed their worries to me about safety issues in Brazil following news reports of police raids into the poorer areas (favelas) and the ongoing street demonstrations involving hundreds of thousands of people. Presented below are tips on survival and health matters in Rio de Janeiro, but many of these are also applicable to other cities throughout Brazil. Most of these tips will not be mentioned in standard tour guidebooks to Brazil, as these have been designed to sell holidays; also, some guides recently published have been written by armchair travellers with little experience of life in Brazil, not by a foreigner actually living there.

Chapter 1

Arrival in Rio

When visiting Brazil, Rio de Janeiro is the place that most people dream of seeing, although the World Cup was held in many different cities in Brazil. Rio is second to São Paulo in size but it is where most large events are staged, such as the recent visit of Pope Francis, games in the World Cup and, of course, the whole of the Olympics in 2016 (except for some of the qualifying games in the football).

Hopefully, you have booked a **direct flight to Rio** and will not arrive via São Paulo. São Paulo airport is often chaotic, with flights to Rio cancelled, delayed for hours or even impossible to find!

Aerial photo of São Paulo, the business capital of Brazil,
but cannot compare to Rio for beauty; also, in the last few years, it has been
experiencing a rapid increase in violent crimes.

From Europe, a British Airways, Air France, TAM or any other airline, direct flight to Rio is highly recommended. BA, however, have adopted a policy of dishing out minimalistic, absolute **rubbish breakfasts** in economy class flights from London, so be prepared to arrive hungry after your flight! Usually, you are allowed two suitcases per person on flights to Rio by BA and TAM (Portuguese airline via Lisbon) but do check this with your airline.

So **avoid São Paulo Airport like the plague**, if possible. Recently, due to cancellation of most GOL flights that day and the next, I waited in vain for hours for a friend to arrive in Rio via São Paulo.I also know of visitors who were misinformed in São Paulo about their connecting gate to Rio and ended up sprinting around São Paulo airport looking for their connecting flights!

After landing in Rio, you then have to pass through long immigration queues and customs. Try to get off the plane **as quickly as possible** and walk rapidly to get to the front of the queue at customs as foreigners are given low priority in comparison with Brazilian travellers. Recently, this situation has greatly improved and now foreigners are being processed more rapidly. **Remember that tourists from European Countries (eg. UK) can stay for 3 months without a visa while the USA and others will need a visa (see: *www.passportvisasexpress.com*). Visas can be renewed for a further 3 months by applying to the Federal Police in the airport (often a long and frustrating business in Galeão International Airport!).**

After customs and baggage collection, and just before you enter the arrivals hall, you will encounter people in official looking booths offering 'safe' taxi vouchers for sale costing about double the normal fares! **Ignore these, as well as the currency exchange booth giving poor rates.** Instead, exit the terminal building, turn right and look for a row of yellow cabs. Inside the cab make sure that the driver has his ID displayed and that the **meter is running** when you drive away. The fare from Rio Galeão International Airport (GIG) to Copacabana should be about 70-85 reais (figure from December 2016), depending upon traffic conditions and time of day, and should take about 40-50 minutes. If you arrive between 4 p.m. and 8 p.m., be prepared for traffic jams. Other popular regions of South Rio, such as Glória, Flamengo and Botafogo, will cost less while Leblon and Ipanema will cost 15-20 reais more. Barra, the past location of the Olympic village, is about 25-30 kilometers from Rio city centre and will cost considerably more at US $50 or 150 reais". Try the Bus Rapid Transit (BRT, blue buses) number 2918 outside both terminals which goes for a few US$ to Alvorado bus terminal in Barra.

If you are on a budget then go to the ground level of the terminal building, exit right and look for the blue bus number 2018 to Copacabana, which leaves every 30 minutes (5 a.m. to 11 p.m.) and costs 15–20 reais (paid to the driver). These, however, take much longer than taxis as they stop everywhere to drop people off. Such buses can be a nightmare as big bags sometimes have to be lifted through the turnstiles on the bus. Do not give the driver large value notes as you may not get your change – they have memory lapses sometimes!

YES, TURNSTILES IN ALL BUSES!

Always bring a few hundred reais (plural of 'real') in 10–50 reais notes and then **change sterling directly** at a *cambio* (the common name for a currency exchange in a travel agent) in the numerous travel agents (often identified outside by "Turismo") around the tourist areas of South Rio. Shop around for the best rate as you can find a lot of variation from one cambio to another. In September 2015, the official exchange rate was 5.9 reais for £1 and I was offered over 6.3 reais on £500. Unfortunately, BREXIT reduced rates to 3.8-4.5 reais for £1. The US dollar is king and you can expect nearly 4 reais per US$1. These exchange rates vary almost daily with the dollar and sterling usually increasing in strength. Withdrawing cash at an ATM can be expensive and your card may be blocked if you have just arrived. This often occurs (especially with NatWest) even if you have told your bank of your planned holiday in Brazil.

'SHOPPING AROUND' is an important rule whether it is for currency, food in supermarkets, pharmacies for basics, or fares in travel agencies. Prices vary hugely even for common items like bananas, mangoes, bread, body creams, shampoos, tissues etc.

The supermarkets often display a cheap deal at the entrances to lure you inside. Since Rio is expensive, if you are staying for an extended period, small savings make a lot of difference to your budget. I recently saved over 1000 reais on a short visit to Buenos Aires. It cost 2,500 reais from my recommended travel agent (below) instead of nearly 3,500 reais from an alternative nearby.

Excellent travel agent: Inovar Turismo, Paulo Rosa (manager),
Avenida N.S. Copacabana 457.

www.inovarturismo.com.br

tel. 21-2256-3595.

Chapter 2

Accommodation

There is some important advice here!!

Many people will probably book a package through an agent in their home country but the following advice is worth reading and is especially useful if you are independent and making your own arrangements.

There are no cheap hotels in Copacabana but there are numerous apartments for rent, usually through agents, but these are not cheap either. Copacabana is very expensive, especially during Carnival and the New Year, so during the Olympics the sky was the limit! During the World Cup, rates at least tripled, although the favourable exchange rates for the dollar and pound will help. Staying outside Copacabana is an option, so study the map of the city and pick places like Botafogo, Flamengo, Laranjeiras or Lapa to stay. Sharing an apartment with friends is an option, as then you can stay on Copacabana; but beware as a deposit will be expected and any defect will be charged. Try ***www.airbnb.com.login*** for reasonable priced accommodation as it works well in Rio with local residents sometimes opening up their homes for rental

THREE POINTS:

i. With a Brazilian agent, you may be given an **incomprehensible contract** in Portuguese to sign so when you move in take photographs of any defects you can find in the apartment – even chipped paint! Before you move out, the apartment will be inspected and any damage will be charged for out of the deposit you have paid. Also, before you move in, ask for an inventory of the contents of the apartment and check these carefully, noting any omissions or damage.

ii. Many apartments have old and dilapidated furniture and equipment so ask whether, if **anything breaks down**, such as the refrigerator, you **will be charged** for repairs. Unbelievably, people renting have been charged hundreds of reais for electrical equipment breakdowns. Also, consumer protection rules do not seem to apply in Brazil, and, as a visitor, you will be unable to pursue your case further. Recently, I rented an apartment in an Apartment Hotel/Hotel Residencia (some rooms are rented as hotel rooms while others are apartments and rented privately, often longer term, by their owners rather than by the hotel) only to have the refrigerator break down soon after I moved in and the agent try to charge me for the repair. Fortunately, the owner visited me, was charming, and soon agreed to pay the bill! I was left wondering whether the agent was trying 'double jeopardy'!

iii. Also, as well as the rent, all apartments have a charge for something called the 'condominium'. I guess this is like the maintenance charge in blocks of flats in the UK. Usually this is included directly in short-term rentals but often is charged separately in longer stays. With most apartments, this may be 300–600 reais per month BUT in Apartment Hotels can be 1,500 reais or more per month. Bottom line: **avoid Apartment Hotels unless you deal directly with the owner or are just renting a hotel room.**

You get very little for your money and at the same time cannot get problems resolved as easily as you can when dealing directly with the owner. The Apartment Hotel reception may tell you that it is not their responsibility despite the fact that you pay so much for the condominium! WHO NEEDS THIS HASSLE ON HOLIDAY!! In my Hotel Residencia, the internet connection is awful so beware if you wish to keep in touch with business or family back home. You will end up sitting in the reception area as this is the only place with Wi-Fi in the hotel and even this breaks down! Recently, after numerous outages, Wi-Fi was installed throughout the building BUT only the hotel guests were allowed usage initially.

Therefore, try to rent an apartment through the owner, rather than an agent, as this will be cheaper. Also, if there are problems then the owner is likely to respond more quickly and cheaply than an agent, especially one based back home. If you can obtain a Sunday copy of the local *O Globo* newspaper, maybe online, then you will find owners renting their apartments directly and can email or phone them. Hopefully, they will speak English, but if not emailing might be better than phoning. Also, contact several other owners that you have seen advertised. There are many agents online but, as expected, their rates are much higher than if you deal with the owner directly. For a short stay, of less than a month, you will probably be charged an inclusive daily rate composed of the rent and condominium combined. For longer stays, you may be able to negotiate for a monthly fee if you deal with the owner.

One hotel in the Copacabana which is comfortable, and good value, is the Royal Rio, ***www.royalrio.com***. It is 5 minutes from the beach, clean, with excellent food and is well serviced. The author has no connection with this hotel but work visitors recommend it. I have eaten there and used the Wi-Fi connection (not to be taken for granted in Brazil!), and am very impressed with the fact that English seems to be the standard language at reception. Unfortunately, during the Carnival etc., I expect that this hotel will be very expensive.

If you are very rich then you must try the famous Copacabana Palace Hotel on the Avenida Atlântica (beach road) as it looks a dream. Normal overnight rates are at least 1,500 reais but such a stay should be outstanding! The hotel runs a special New Year Ball which costs over 2000 reais per ticket but is fabulous by all accounts. Reservations: 0845 0772 222

The magnificent Copacabana Palace Hotel

Chapter 3

Banks

These can be an **ABSOLUTE NIGHTMARE** in Rio!

- All ATMs are inside the banks and not on the street BUT at any one time many of these may not function. Occasionally, none or few of the ATM machines will dispense money in one or more of the local branches of the Bank of Brazil in Copacabana.

- During local holidays, there are strict limits on the amount of money that you can withdraw and this can be as low as 300 reais, or only about £50 or US$75, for the weekend. Therefore always stockpile some money before a holiday and for the weekend.

Bank of Brazil ATM terminal in maintenance

- The top **daily limit on a card is usually 1,000 reais, or about £165 or US$ 250**, so paying rents in cash is a problem. On weekdays, more money can be withdrawn by queuing up to see the counter staff within the bank through the armed guards and security scans. However, you will need a passport and may still be refused as you do not have an account in the bank! I have been refused both to open an account and to send a Western Union message from the Banco de Brasil, near Rua Siqueira Campos, Copacabana despite having all the necessary paperwork.

- This top limit of **1,000 reais is supposed to last you all the weekend and sometimes Monday** as well.

- The ATM machines shut down at 10 p.m. (22.00 hours), so late withdrawals are not usually possible. Also, your card may be refused even though you enter all the correct passwords for your account. Try moving to different ATM machines and you may be lucky!

- Finally, do not be surprised if your **bank blocks your card the first time you use it in an ATM in Brazil**, so have your bank's emergency phone number at hand. The NatWest bank regularly blocks my Visa card on my return to Rio from the UK, despite the fact I tell the bank that I am travelling abroad to Rio on a certain day! Routinely, test your card immediately upon arrival in Rio so you can live on your cash until it is unblocked. Maybe your apartment will not have an effective internet connection so you will have to find an internet café or use an iPhone, if you have one, to contact your bank.

- **YES, do take cash for changing into reais but keep this safe and hidden away (even if staying in a hotel room)** or in a hotel safe box. The rate of exchange in cambios (exchanges) in travel agencies is optimal and you avoid nightmare ATM machines and bank charges.

- Hopefully, your VISA, Mastercard etc will not be blocked and you can withdraw money at the ATM machines with the CIRRUS emblem showing. The HSBC bank ATMs seem to be the best in terms of the amount you can withdraw, and will allow you the full daily limit of 1000 reais.

Chapter 4

Getting Around

There are yellow cabs everywhere in Rio and they are easy to stop, except when it rains. Always ensure that the meter is turned on and make a note of your route as you do not want a city tour! Brazil is a Catholic country and taxis displaying a crucifix on the mirror seem to be the most reliable. A small tip (2–3 reais) is appreciated and most cab drivers are helpful although sometimes the same route costs different amounts!

Take care with the local buses

Buses are very frequent, fast and cover the whole city, but **can be dangerous** so the superb **Rio Metro is recommended** and is cheap at 3–4 reais. The range of the Metro, however, is limited, but it is rapidly expanding and now covers more of Rio, including the Maracana stadium and Barra. Look in any Metro stop for a map of the main lines. Other railways seem to be underused, with many railway lines apparently ripped up years ago to provide routes for new roads. It was 20 years before I saw my first train!

A WARNING ABOUT THE RIO BUSES! If you are elderly, at all frail or with small children then avoid them. Many of the buses are driven by frustrated racing drivers and as soon as you enter they accelerate away at high speed to throw you into the turnstile or onto the lap of another passenger! The fare is less than £1, i.e. 3-4 reais for any location in Rio, but try to have the right money as you will be hanging on for dear life! Many buses do not have air conditioning, which makes the journey unpleasant in the summer (November to March). Another very serious problem is the fact that **there are no limits on passenger numbers** so that in rush hours the buses often carry hugely excessive and dangerous loads of people.

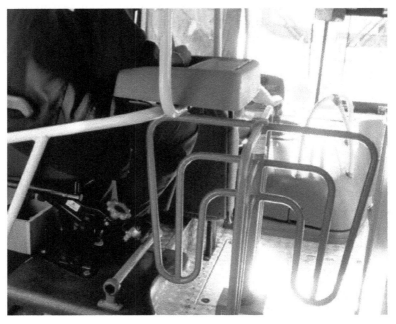

The dreaded turnstile upon boarding a local Rio bus.

This, coupled with an outside temperature of 37–38ºC, is unbearable, especially for new arrivals from colder climates. I know of local people who refuse to use the buses at all.

The bus stops in Copacabana and elsewhere in Rio need explaining. The bus stops are labelled 1, 2, or 3 and the windscreens of the buses also display a number 1, 2 or 3 to indicate which bus stops they use. There is a blue table at each bus stop showing which number buses stop at bus stops 1, 2 and 3 and their destinations (See photo).

Do not expect people to queue for buses as it is a free-for-all once the bus stops. If you are young and fit you will soon get the hang of the push and shove to enter the bus!

Bus stop. Buses showing 3 on the windscreen stop here.
Also, note the blue table of bus destinations.

Other buses are available for long distance travel and these are run by the 1001 company in Rio and by other companies elsewhere, and are excellent. They are much more comfortable than National Express (UK), with plenty of leg room and air conditioning. Their charges are also reasonable with a 3 hour journey of about 200 km costing around £25 return. The 1001 buses leave from the Rio **Central Bus Station, called the *Rodoviaria Novo Rio*,** near the Avenida Brasil. It is better to get a taxi to this station as the buses from Copacabana take ages and go around the moon in the city centre. If you have plenty of time and courage then buses 126, 127 and 128 go to the Central Bus Station.

The 1001 buses go to all cities around Rio de Janeiro and to many other places, including São Paulo and beauty spots like Búzios, once frequented by Brigitte Bardot. All fares can be bought online in English simply by entering '1001 buses' into ***www.google.com.br.*** If you use the official website it may be difficult to find the section in English. Alternatively, the bus station, which is new, is well organised and serviced, so you could just turn up and buy a ticket. If you understand Portuguese you can buy tickets at ***www.buscaonibus.com.br***

ANOTHER WARNING concerns an alternative form of transport, the **transit vans**, which were once found throughout Rio but have been banned in many districts now. These are often unlicensed and again pile in passengers to really dangerous levels, with people standing with no chance of surviving in an accident. Unaccompanied girls should also avoid these at all costs. These vans still exist in some areas of Rio but it is probably best to take some other form of transport.

FINAL COMMENT ON BUSES

There is about to be a major reorganisation of the bus routes in parts of Rio to reduce the number in Copacabana and lower pollution and noise levels so look out for new details in the bus stops.

Chapter 5

Food and Restaurants

Food in Brazil can be of a very high standard with a good choice of fruit and vegetables, but you have to know what to eat and where to go.

To appreciate the range of fruit and vegetables, visit a supermarket or even the Sunday Market in Copacabana (Rua Hilário de Gouvêia, Sundays until 2 p.m.). Frankly, **I have limited the use of this market as the food is exposed to the heat for hours and not that cheap.** Also, the area around the market attracts unsavoury characters who sell fruit and vegetables left over from the market and will rip you off. Make sure that you know the value of the note you pay them with as they may distract you and claim that your 50 reais note was only 2 reais!!!!! I use the market just for vegetables and a few items of fruit, such as mangoes, *mamão formosa, mamão papaia* (papaya) and tomatoes. Grapes and bananas can be expensive and of poor value.

Look at your currency notes in reais and see that the 2 and 100 reais notes are both blue, so take care! Never pull out 50 or 100 reais notes in the market but carry plenty of 2 and 5 reais notes and change.

There are two types of restaurant to try initially:

1. The buffet restaurants. These are marvellous and can often be identified by a price notice outside giving the price per 100 grams (g) of food (see photo). This price should be 4-6 reais at present in Copacabana. Inside the restaurant, you will be given a slip of paper and find a buffet of maybe 20 to 50 different foods ranging through salads, meats, fruits, vegetables, rice, pasta, sweets and a barbecue. All you have to do is fill your plate with what you want and have it weighed, handing over your paper for stamping with the price.

Part of a typical buffet restaurant often with a huge choice of foods.

For a man, 500–900 g is usually plenty, and for women, probably, less than this! This is an excellent system as you only pay for the amount of food that you actually take, which varies greatly between the different family members. The first time people use the buffet, they often put too much food on an enormous plate, but they soon adjust! One of the best restaurants at a very reasonable price is the Siqueira Grill in Rua Siqueira Campos, Copacabana. An outstanding meal for a man here will cost 50-60 reais, or £12-15 or US$ 15-17, but for children and for those that eat less it will be much cheaper. Other fine restaurants are in the 'Aipo & Aipim' chain.

Outside a buffet restaurant displaying the price of the food
per 100 grams (4.09–4.39 reais) or for
'All You Can Eat' at 26.90 reais (now 32 reais).

2. The barbecue restaurants (*churrascarias*) are unbelievable and strictly for non-vegetarians! Inside, you will find a help yourself salad bar. When you sit down, suddenly waiters with long knives will arrive, one after another, bearing a bewildering array of meats. It is up to you to select which meats you want until you have had enough and can eat no more. Some restaurants have a red or green flag on the table and the meats will continue to arrive as long as you show the green flag, only stopping when you surrender with the red flag!

Churrascaria Palace (Carvery) Restaurant (highly recommended). Rua Rodolfo Dantas 16, around the corner from the Copacabana Palace Hotel

Unfortunately, Brazil, together with India and China, is being targeted by the big multinational purveyors of junk food because markets in the Western World are no longer expanding due to the financial recession. The end result in Rio is that obesity is becoming rife. **Why buy such junk as chips, hamburgers and other high calorific food when Brazil has such a quantity of fantastic fruit and vegetables to try??** Again, avoid the junk food by going to the buffet restaurants (from which you can take out food) or for self-catering just visit the local supermarket and buy your own food.

Many restaurants also do **'Executive Menus'** at lunchtime at very reasonable prices. The idea is to provide a quick, wholesome meal for the busy worker. Look for the Executive Menu often advertised outside the restaurant. La Mole restaurant chain does a special lunch menu at a very reasonable price of 25–35 reais, but this will vary according to whereabouts you are in Rio.

A typical Suco Bar with a huge range of freshly blended fruit drinks available.

You must also try a Suco Bar (Juice Bar), which serves a multitude of fruit juices for £2–3 and is found on many street corners. They have fantastic displays of different fruits and you can buy exotic concoctions to wake you up and invigorate you.

Try the *prato de verão* at the Big B Sucos chain, which will cost 13–15 reais and provide enough whole fresh fruit for two!

Finally, if you are catering for yourself then some health tips related to the food are given below in chapter 7 **'Staying Healthy'**. Also, see the following website for details of a healthy lifestyle: ***www.endtheconfusion.wordpress.com***

Chapter 6

Staying Safe

There is no need to worry unduly about safety in Rio, providing you read and follow the advice below. This advice is the same as people would sensibly follow in any large city although some extra vigilance is advisable in Rio.

Safety is a priority concern for people thinking about visiting Rio and Brazil. The recent unrest and demonstrations even threatened the viability of the World Cup and Olympics according to the press. The World Cup, however, was on schedule and demonstrations sizzled to nothing in the winter sun! There are many injustices in Brazilian society and the people are finally showing their impatience with the slow progress of change. However, people were sufficiently proud of their country and did not threaten the Olympics to the extent that they were moved to another country. Even so, the demonstrations have not threatened the safety of ordinary people so travellers should not be concerned about this. However, if the people do not see some progress then their thoughts may be directed to further disruption. The increase in bus and boat fares, which triggered the demonstrations, were **cancelled very soon after the unrest began** but this will be insufficient to satisfy people in the long term.

Another problem now is that the Brazilian economy, based largely on commodities, has failed to maintain the momentum of 2007–8. This situation has been made worse by corruption and the disappearance of billions of Petrobras oil dollars. This has resulted in serious Government cutbacks in the universities and across the board. Inevitably, poorer people are suffering and more appear to be sleeping on the streets now. This has already led to further mass demonstrations with the President Dilma Rousseff having been impeached and removed from office.

Other concerns include robberies, kidnappings and petty thieving, as well as rapes. Copacabana and surrounding areas often lack policing so that such events are on the increase especially in the poorer areas (the shanty town districts, called *favelas*) which should be avoided, especially at night.

Now and again, however, as in Xmas 2013 and September 2015, there were mass raids on the beaches of Ipanema and Copacabana with gangs of youngsters running along the beaches stealing handbags etc. Now 6,000 more police have been assigned to the area. Even so, no valuables should ever be taken onto the beach. Use common sense – so **no expensive jewellery or large amounts of cash should be carried or worn**. Occasionally, groups of very lively young boys/teenagers are seen running around the streets, wearing just shorts and making a lot of noise. These are probably from poorer areas and on the lookout for easy money from soft targets. Cross over the street and avoid them if possible. Sometimes (especially on Sundays in Copacabana) gangs of youths gather at bus stops trying to get free bus rides when the rear doors open. Simply walk to another bus stop to avoid this problem and never get on a bus filled with noisy youths.

It is not advisable for women to go out unaccompanied at night. Recently, an English girl staying in a hostel in Copacabana went out alone at night, it began to rain, a man offered to share his umbrella and then pushed her into an alley and tried to rape her. Rapes have also occurred in the transit vans, mentioned in Chapter 4, but rest assured that these are not common events if you follow my advice above.

Another point to remember is that the **zebra crossings on all the roads DO NOT GIVE pedestrians the right of way.** Wait for the lights to change to green on the crossing and, before stepping out, look right to confirm that nobody is **JUMPING THE LIGHTS, BUT THEN ALSO LEFT as many cyclists move against the flow of traffic**, often with loads of water bottles or crates of shopping. Finally, if you do cross on a red light then use both your eyes and ears as **high-speed motorbikes** are increasing in numbers and there appears to be no check on their speed or death rates of the riders at present.

When walking along the **pot-holed and dangerous pavements**, if you hear a high-pitched beeping and see a flashing orange light outside a building then beware; it means that any moment a car will appear from a subterranean car park and cross the pavement (see photo).

Finally, **beware some shoe-shine boys** as they can be very persistent and try to shine even your sandals. Recently, one cleaned the shoes of a naïve visitor before he negotiated a price, and the boy wanted 30 reais (5–6 is normal)!! They have all sorts or tricks so take care.

Car driving across pavement to enter subterranean car park

Chapter 7

Staying Healthy

All visitors should see their doctor and be immunized against yellow fever and influenza. Generally however, there are a few health issues not found at home and others that are found at home but claim more victims in Rio, as follows:

i. **Parasitic diseases**, including **Dengue** and the new, much publicized, rapidly spreading **Zika virus** occur mainly in the cities such as Rio and are transmitted by mosquitoes. Some of these mosquitoes can be recognised by their striped bodies like tigers (see photo).

Dengue and Zika are more common in the height of the summer and the rainy season from January to February each year, including both the New Year and Carnival. Another virus causing concern, but less common and transmitted by the same mosquito, *Aedes aegypti,* responsible for Zika and Dengue, is Chikungunya. Simple ways of reducing being bitten by mosquitoes include:-

- Using repellents, such as oil of lemon eucalyptus or EPA registered repellents, on skin and clothes but not on children less than 3 yr old. EPA registered chemical repellents are also available, such as Deet that can be used on the skin (check label) and children if diluted to less than 30%. Wash hands after use.

- Using insect repelling wrist and ankle bands

- Shutting windows and use air conditioning especially around dusk

- Wearing light coloured clothes

- Staying in a high level room

- Care in toilets and lifts often with trapped mosquitoes

- If pregnant cover up and avoid infected countries

- If pregnant avoid sex with infected partner/use condoms

- Getting rid of standing water, plastic cups and alcohol remnants in glasses.

(see: ***http://www.cdc.gov/features/stopmosquitoes/***)

Most people have no symptoms of Zika infection although aches, pains and a raging fever accompany Dengue fever and merit consulting a doctor **using your travel insurance, which you must have**. Concern with Zika is the incidence of microcephaly in babies born to infected mothers. Some forms of Dengue cause serious symptoms of bleeding and even death occasionally. A dengue vaccine has been produced and a Zika vaccine will probably be available in a few years. Tourists should not be complacent about these diseases but take appropriate precautions, outlined above. Alternatively, since there were few if any such infections in the World Cup or Olympics then visiting in the winter months July to September is a safe option".

Anti-malarial pills are not required in Rio or further south but Northern and Western Brazil, including Manaus, Porto Velho and Macapá, especially in the Amazonia, still have cases of malaria.

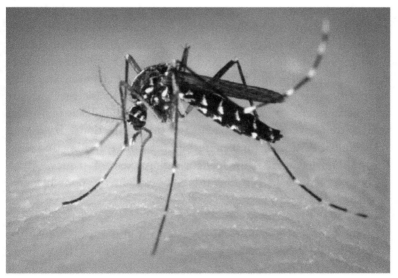

Aedes albopictus female mosquito taking a blood meal from a human host. This mosquito can transmit the virus causing Dengue Fever in Rio and elsewhere. It can also bite at any time of the day.
Note the characteristic stripes. James Gathany/CDC.

This image is a work of the Centers for Disease Control, part of the United States Department of Health and Human Services, taken or made as part of an employee's official duties. As a work of the U.S. Federal Government, the image is in the public domain.

The other dangerous parasite in Brazil is **Leishmania** transmitted by sand flies (even smaller than mosquitoes!) and, although not a problem in the cities, it is widespread especially in the states of Minas Gerais and Pará in poorer areas.

ii. **Other infectious diseases common in Rio** and elsewhere are **colds and flu**. These are often transmitted by hand contact with door handles, money etc. and can ruin a holiday. Unfortunately, many Brazilians do not use tissues to wipe their noses and whatever emerges contaminates other people in enclosed spaces in buses, restaurants etc. to infect other people. The frequent use of alcohol hand gel and thorough hand washing is highly recommended after travelling anywhere and before food. Many buffet restaurants have alcohol hand gel dispensers. Always make up a basic first aid box with plasters, throat spray, paracetamol, Lemsip and scissors. I also pack antibiotics against toothache and other infections. Try asking your dentist or doctor for a prescription before travelling and keep the pills refrigerated. Also, bring small packets of tissues, which are very expensive in Rio and this may explain the poor hygiene, described above.

Using taxis and not buses or the Metro is also a way of avoiding colds and flu from sneezing and coughing people. If planning to stay in Rio for 1 year or more then having a flu vaccination is recommended.

iii. **Food poisoning** can occur although certain precautions can be taken to minimise incidences. DO NOT DRINK THE TAP WATER but use bottled water. Avoid mayonnaise dishes like potato salad. Always wash salad items in diluted (few drops to a bowl of water) *agua sanitaria*, which you can buy in any supermarket; rinse thoroughly and dry. If you have a bad tummy then keep well hydrated and try using a local Brazilian remedy called **Floratil**, which is wonderful and harmless and can be bought from any *pharmacia* (chemist). The ice creams and cakes are fine to eat occasionally!!

iv. **Beware the sun in the November to April** period as it can be in the upper 30°Cs to the 40°Cs in Rio and elsewhere so always protect your skin and use factor 30–50 sun cream. Sunglasses should also always be worn, regardless of the time of the year and even if it is cloudy.

v. Also, beware of **numerous potholes** in pavements and roads which are far worse than at home. Even so many women still manage to wear high heels!

Chapter 8

Getting Help

This can be very frustrating as the average person in the street understands very little English and is often not willing to try. The best people to approach are the young, well dressed people as learning English is now recognised as a top priority and they can be very helpful indeed. If you are hurt then people will assist you. Clinics abound but again **you must have travel insurance to cover the costs.** There are public hospitals but queues are long and without Portuguese it will be difficult to progress. Do not try complaining to anybody if something goes wrong (except to your agent or landlord about your apartment) as this is not the way Brazilians operate and may explain the frustration being expressed in the present demonstrations. ALWAYS CARRY A PHOTOCOPY OF YOUR PASSPORT (leaving the original in your safe with your other valuables), JUST IN CASE THERE IS AN EMERGENCY. **You can always go directly to the British Consulate in Praia Flamengo for help, although now you are supposed to have an appointment.** If you turn up unannounced and knock on the door with your passport then you may be successful in getting help although this will be impossible during major events. The above advice applies to all nationalities visiting Brazil and their consulates/embassies.

Useful telephone numbers and contacts are given below:

- To book bus trips on the 1001 line: ***www.buscaonibus.com.br***

- Good hotel: the Royal Rio, ***www.royalrio.com***

- Excellent travel agent: Inovar Turismo, Paulo Rosa (manager), Avenida N.S. Copacabana 457. ***www.inovarturismo.com.br*** Tel. 21-2256-3595. He speaks perfect English and is open Monday–Saturday. He can book you trips to tropical islands or to Búzios, a popular resort 3 hours from Rio.

- Tourism Police: 21-3399-7171.

- British Consulate: Praia do Flamengo, 284 - Flamengo, Rio de Janeiro - RJ, 22210-030. Tel. 21-2555-9600. Appointments needed but may respond to a visit by knocking on the door. Take your passport! E-mail: ***bcg.rj@fco.gov.uk***

- U.S. Consulate for emergencies include death, arrest, stolen or lost passports. US Consulate General Rio de Janeiro, Av. Presidente Wilson, 147 Castelo RJ - 20030-020, Rio de Janeiro, RJ (entrance at Rua Santa Luzia). For 24 hour emergency help, during Consulate's working hours (8 a.m. to 5 p.m.), tel. 21- 3823-2000; outside these working hours, please only call, 21-3823-2029. An appointment will be required. E-mail: ***acsrio@state.gov***.

- MAB's restaurant, Av. Atlântica, 1140, Copacabana.

- Emergency ambulance: tel. 192 (but this will take you to a public hospital).

- Emergency private ambulance: 21-2257-3848, but these can be hugely expensive and can charge ridiculous prices for foreigners. Try to take a Brazilian friend with you to the private hospital to ensure that you are not charged too much. The Hospital Copa D'Or in Rua Siqueira Campos tried to charge an American friend of mine several thousand reais for taking him to a private hospital in Ipanema, a short drive away.

- For cardiac emergency: 21-2527-6060.

- If staying in a hotel and requiring a doctor then simply phone reception and they should help. If in an apartment, then just walk around Copacabana and look for one of the many private clinics who should help you, BUT you must have travel insurance to cover the costs. If you forgot to take out health insurance before you travelled then consult Inovar Turismo, Paulo Rosa (manager), Avenida N.S. Copacabana 457. *__www.inovarturismo.com.br__* Tel. 21-2256-3595 and they can help you get cover.

NB: A friend recently had a painful incidence with gall stones and went to one of the pre-hospital emergency units, called UPAs. This unit was found in Copacabana, right in front of the Siqueira Campos Metrô exit. It was clean, efficient, free and open 24 hr. Another unit can be found in Botafogo where Rua São Clemente meets Rua Nelson Mandela 10, close to the Botafogo Metrô station.

Chapter 9

The Weather

The **Carnival** occurs in Rio and elsewhere in Brazil during February or March each year, which is in **the summer** and the rainy season with temperatures often in the 30°Cs or even 40°Cs for days on end. Only basic shorts and tops are required due to the heat which can make sleeping very difficult. Most accommodation should have air conditioning but it is worth checking on this before you move in. This is also the time for Zika and Dengue fever so take care, as in Chapter 7, to avoid being bitten by mosquitoes which transmit the disease

There was, however, very little rain in Brazil during January and February 2015 but, surprisingly, Dengue fever levels increased over 200% in 2016, between January and May, compared with the same period in 2015. Over 50% of the cases were in São Paulo due to the storage of water in open containers in which the mosquitoes bred massively.

The **World Cup and the Olympics/Paralympics**, took place in the **Brazilian winter**, during June to September when temperatures are cooler, in the 20°Cs usually, and the weather is very similar (but normally much drier!) to the British summer and can be chilly at night. **Make sure that you bring an umbrella and some warm clothing in the winter, such as a dressing gown, as most accommodation lacks any heating**. The sun often shines in Rio in the winter and is the safest time to go to the beach and avoid the ravages of the sun and mosquito bites.

Chapter 10

Places to Visit in Rio and Elsewhere

The following are very famous in Rio:

i. **The statue of Jesus Christ or Christ the Redeemer**, or Corcovado (the mountain on which the statue is built) as it is sometimes called. This is one of the Seven Wonders of the World and is well worth a visit. The statue is 125 feet high and the views of Rio from the statue base are outstanding. The commonest way of getting up to the statue is on the railway but queues are very long so get there early. Opening times are 8 a.m. until 6 p.m. and the cost is 40-50 reais, about US$14-15, 13 euros or £10-12. There is a bus, the 593, which goes from Copacabana to Cosme Velo but again only if you are young and fit! Families should go by taxi; although hotels arrange visits they are expensive. Recently, a new service has opened on the Avenida Atlântica (the beach road) at the Praça do Lido, a small park not far from the Copacabana Palace Hotel.

Jesus Christ or Christ the Redeemer Statue (Corcovado)
Photo courtesy of Professor Cicero Brasileiro

Lido Park where you can buy tickets for visiting the Christ the Redeemer statue

In the Lido Park, you can buy tickets at about 50–60 reais (free for up to 5 year olds) and then join the queue outside the park for a van to drive you to see the statue. This is a good and comfortable return service which is non-stop to see the statue (see photo). It operates 8 a.m. to 5 p.m. but arrive early to avoid queues. Once at the base of the statue, there are steps to climb but disabled people can use a lift.

View of Rio from the statue of Jesus Christ

ii. **The Sugar Loaf Mountain (Pão de Açúcar)**. This is a fun trip and involves two cable car rides to the top. Opening times are 8 a.m. to 8 p.m. and prices are 60–75 reais for adults and half that for children. The Sugar Loaf is very near to Copacabana so a taxi fare should not be expensive, although again a bus, number 581, could be used from Copacabana or Ipanema.

Sugar Loaf Mountain

iii. **The Maracanã Stadium** is well worth a visit to see the local football teams play and enjoy the enthusiasm of the supporters. A ticket can be bought through a travel agent or a hotel and should cost no more than 120 reais. This stadium was used for the Olympics. The surrounding area is not that secure so an organised trip, costing more, with a guide is recommended.

The Maracanã Stadium

iv. **The Carnival parade**. This is a must to see the most amazing and enormous floats which parade hour upon hour through the Rio Carnival **Sambadrome**. Again, visit this with an organized trip using a guide to help you find your way through the crowds. Practically every street in Rio will celebrate the Carnival but this will mainly consist of excessive drinking and dancing day after day.

v. **Other sites which are free in Rio** include the famous Copacabana and Ipanema beaches (see photo of Copacabana Beach) on which about 40 reais will pay for an umbrella, lounger and beer).

Aerial view of Copacabana beach, February 2011.
By Gustavo Facci from Argentina (Copacabana)
*[CC BY-SA 2.0 (**http://creativecommons.org/licenses/by-sa/2.0**)],*
via Wikimedia Commons

The Girl from Ipanema (Garota de Ipanema) restaurant is a real waste of time and on a very noisy road. Real fun is to stroll by the Copacabana beach on a Sunday to take in the sights and sounds; the Avenida Atlântica is closed to traffic and everybody goes to the beach or exercises by strolling, running or biking. Also, there are many small cafes at the edge of the beach serving a variety of food and drink, including the famous *caipirinhas*.

At the north end of the beach is the **Windsor Hotel** and as you walk towards Ipanema to the south you will pass the many restaurants, including, the **MAB's and La Maison restaurants**, with cheap executive lunches (weekdays). Restaurants are few in number on Leblon and Ipanema beaches. At the south end of the Copacabana beach is the **Sofitel Hotel**, just before Leblon and Ipanema beaches. These latter beaches tend to attract the beautiful, and sometimes rich, people of Rio. The roads leading from Leblon and Ipanema beaches contain a whole variety of high-class restaurants, bars and nightclubs and are well worth exploring. Look at ***www.gringo-rio*.** com/ for information on bars, restaurants and nightlife in Rio. This website is very useful for additional information on Rio but lacks many aspects of the advice given in the present book.

It is also worth visiting the **Flea Market in Ipanema** on Sundays for souvenirs, as well as the famous **Selaron Steps in Lapa** (buses 433 and 464 from Copacabana). Lapa is also where a whole range of nightclubs can be found, catering for every taste in music – samba, reggae and pop – but get there early (before 8 p.m.) to avoid the queues.

The famous tiled steps in Lapa with the artistic creator, Selaron (RIP)

Romantic trips to Búzios (a favourite of Brigitte Bardot) are highly recommended at about 100 miles from Rio with beautiful beaches and hotels. Again through a travel agent or hotel these could be expensive but can be booked online and a car hired for the trip. This little paradise may be very expensive and crowded during the Olympics and Carnival with local Brazilians fleeing from Rio!

Statue of Brigitte Bardot, Búzios beach, Rio de Janeiro,
By Chistina Motta (São Paulo, 1944) (Own work) [Public domain], via Wikimedia Commons

vi. **A fine and cheap trip** is to take the boat (barca) from Praça Quinze, near Rio city centre, to Niteroi. Praça Quinze is about 20 reais in a taxi from Copacabana and the return boat fare less than 10 reais. The trip gives you wonderful views of Rio and of the bridge connecting Rio city centre with Niteroi. On your return trip, take a bus (1001, number 2470) from Niteroi to Copacabana and sit on the right side of the bus and you will be looking down 50–100 feet from the bridge directly into the sea from your seat! This bus is a different line from the lunatic buses in Copacabana!

Ferry boat from Praça Quinze with Sugar Loaf in the background

vii. **Trips outside Rio** can be arranged if you are staying longer in Brazil. I especially recommend:

• Iguassu Falls, between Brazil and Argentina, which are higher than Niagara and can be accessed from Rio by plane. Take your passport and you can cross into Argentina one evening and try a fabulous steak.

Iguassu Falls

- The Amazon Rainforest in the north of Brazil is astonishing and a wonderful experience. The north-east of Brazil also has some beautiful resorts like Fortaleza and Natal and the famous Opera House in Manaus.

- In fact, Brazil has so many wonderful places to visit that you will be spoilt for choice so consult an excellent travel agent: Inovar Turismo, Paulo Rosa, Avenida N.S. Copacabana 457. ***www.inovarturismo.com.br***, tel. 21-2256-3595 if in Rio. He will also help you with advice on the Carnival.

- Finally, Buenos Aires is a wonderful and vibrant city and **extremely cheap at the present time** due to the strength of the dollar and pound against the Argentinian peso. Stay in the Recoleta district, go shopping, try the steaks and see a tango show. Some shows are free in the parks in the evening and you can try it yourself, but do not forget a small tip for your tango partner! No special paperwork, except a passport, is required to enter Argentina.

viii. **Cultural centres**

The Centre of Rio has many cultural sites of interest including theatres, museums and palaces. Particularly noteworthy are i. The Teatro Municipal (see photo, Municipal Theatre, for ballet and classical music), ii. The Biblioteca Nacional do Brasil (The National Library, the largest library in South America), and iii. The Museu do Amanhã (see photo, Museum of Tomorrow), a modern architectural miracle. The Museum of Tomorrow, located near the City Centre at Plaça Mauá, opened in 2015, deals with sustainability and climate and population changes. It is expected to be one of the top attractions in Rio in the future. In addition, the Contemporary Art Museum is also located across the bay in Niteroi and a wonderful example of the work of the famous Brazilian architect Oscar Niemeyer.

Municipal Theatre in Rio City Centre

"Museum of Tomorrow" Science Museum

"Museum of Tomorrow" Science Museum

There are many guided tours of these cultural sites but if you are brave and can arrive in the City Centre (by bus or Metro) in Avenida Rio Branco then there is a modern tram service (VLT, light rail) that will take you past the Municipal Theatre, the National Library at Cinelândia and the Museum of Tomorrow at Plaça Mauá. This same VLT also connects with the Rio downtown Airport at Santos Dumont".

Rio VLT tram service

Chapter 11

Carnival and New Year Celebrations

New Year on Copacabana Beach, 2004,

The Brazilians love a party and this is illustrated twice a year on a massive scale with the New Year (Reveillon) and Carnival celebrations throughout Rio and in most towns in Brazil.

DO REMEMBER THAT THE NEW YEAR AND THE CARNIVAL ARE BOTH HELD IN THE BRAZILIAN SUMMER WHEN DENGUE AND ZIKA VIRUSES ARE INCREASING IN NUMBER DUE TO THE HOT AND MOIST CONDITIONS FAVOURING MOSQUITOES (see Chapter 7 on how to avoid mosquito bites).

There is no need to cancel your visit and can monitor the incidences of these diseases in Rio and elsewhere by logging into ***http://www.travelvax.com.au/travel-health-alerts*** for update information, and into the Centre for Disease Control, USA, at ***http://www.cdc.gov/features/stopmosquitoes/***, for more details on the use of repellents against mosquitoes etc.

New Year

For the New Year on the Copacabana, several million people gather dressed in white to watch the fireworks display. Most hotels are fully booked and many people carry bottles of champagne to open as 12 o'clock arrives. Offshore, beautiful cruise ships covered in lights anchor to watch the fireworks and the 4-5 kilometer beach is filled with joyful people full of hope for the New Year. On the beach, opposite the iconic Copacabana Palace Hotel, a stage is erected and various pop groups wow the audience while the New Year approaches. The problem is that it is most difficult to walk anywhere near this area due to the crowds and it is not recommended for the very young or frail.

There are several ways to watch the New Year celebrations and fireworks that are set off from barges offshore:

- The cheap way by pushing through the crowds to stand near or on the beach amongst the other several million people. Beware of pick pockets but usually safe with the option of buying beer/water from vendors.

- To buy tickets for a celebration meal and drink in one of the many restaurants on the Avenida Atlantica. These restaurants erect safety barriers around the tables and chairs at the front to protect the clients from the crowds and are policed by security. The tickets vary in price, depending on demand, but protection is provided for clients from the crush and allow them to enjoy a civilised meal and drink. Two such restaurants are La Maison and MABS but there are many more.

- If you are not on a budget then booking into a hotel overlooking the beach is optimal. Many have swimming pools and viewing terraces on the top floors and will provide a very special night away from the crowds to view the spectacle below. Very expensive but well worth it for this occasion. Many hotels also have New Year parties without the need to book a room for overnight. Examples are the Marriott and Hotel Pestano but you will need to contact the hotel and book well in advance.

My ultimate (one for my bucket list!) would be to go to the Copacabana Palace Hotel with a wonderful terrace on the lower floors overlooking the beach. Such an occasion would create an unforgettable memory of a fabulous evening but at a price of US$1100-1500 for a New Year party ticket with dinner, band and outstanding views *__http://maninrio.com/product/new-years-eve-dinner-package-copacabana-palace-rio-de-jan__*.

Finally, many apartments overlooking the Copacabana beach are available for rental. For the New Year, the rates would be at least R$1,200 + per person or £300 or US$250 for 4 days *__https://www.airbnb.com/rooms/295383__*. This is very good value for such an iconic event and would be ideal for a group of friends.

NB: Do remember that after the New Year celebrations if you are not staying somewhere near the Copacabana Beach then transport will be difficult to find to take you home, although the Metro has been running in recent years but with huge queues.

Carnival

The Rio Carnival is probably the most famous such event in the whole world. The dates for the Carnival are set each year at about 40 days before Easter and are in:

i. 2017, 24th February to 1st March, with the winners' parade on Saturday March 4th.

ii. 2018, 9th February to 13th February, with the winners' parade on Saturday February 17th.

Although, officially, the Carnival only lasts 5 days, in fact, it seems to go on for weeks! Thus, after the last carnival day of 1st March in 2017, only three days later, there is the parade in the *Sambadrome* of the winners of the *Samba School* floats. The samba schools also provide evening events for tourists for some months before the Carnival which can be booked with transport through a travel agent for about 120 reais. One such samba school providing a pre-taste of the carnival is Mangueira, the winners of the 2016 parade. For safety, since many of the samba schools are based in poorer areas, then it is wise to visit a school with the good security such as Mangueira.

In addition to the famous samba school parades in the *Sambadrome*, there are also numerous street parties throughout Rio. If you cannot make the official carnival dates then walk down the Avenida Atlantica in Copacabana on Sundays, after the New Year at about 4pm, and listen, watch and join in the rehearsal parades of the street party samba bands. Alternatively, follow your ears and you will soon locate the beat and excitement of other street parties to join.

The sambadrome is actually a stretch of the Avenida Marquês de Sapucaí cordoned off and with massive concrete stands erected each side, like an elongated football stadium, along which the floats of the samba schools parade for about 6-9 hr each night (see figure with green giant). Each school parades for about 80 min in the sambadrome and adopts a different theme each year.

Carnival parade in sambadrome Rio de Janeiro, performers from the Rio Portela samba school, 2016. This float is enormous and gives some idea of the size and dedication involved in producing these floats.

Googleimage. Date: 2016-02-05.
http://www.theworldfestival.net/rio-carnival-image-gallery.html
Permission requested

The various samba schools are social clubs representing various neighbourhoods of Rio and spend much of the year with skilled workers in building the amazing floats. Each school has fans and supporters like a football club and the competition to win the parade is intense. There are over 70 samba schools in Rio alone, some with full-time designers employed and 1500 members too. The schools also belong to leagues and can be promoted or relegated, depending on the scores awarded after the parade. Every year 40 judges pick a group of 6 schools from which to find a winner on the Saturday parade in the sambadrome after the carnival.

Carnival in Rio de Janeiro, photo by Sergio Luiz 2006 (own work)
[Public Domain], under the Creative Commons Attribution 2.0 Generic License,
via Wikimedia Commons

Due to the crowds on each day making their way to the sambadrome, I would recommend buying the carnival tickets from a reputable agent and include transport and a guide to and from the stadium. This is fine if you are already in Rio but otherwise you will need to buy the tickets online at, for example, **_www.carnivalbookers.com/Carnival-Rio_** (with whom I have no experience). Apparently, the tickets sometimes take some time to arrive, so book early or get a friend in Rio to do this if possible. Also, the location of your seat is important and in the middle of section 5 is recommend as it is cheaper and used by local people rather than tourists. Also, high seats give you better views, as many floats are enormous, than sitting down low next to the parade. Remember to take plenty of insect repellent, water and food as you maybe on your feet dancing for 8 hours! Arrive at 8pm, one hour before the start in order to guarantee your seat or otherwise it is first come first served.

Another possibility is to attend a *Carnival Ball* located in various parts of the city with the rich going to the Copacabana Palace for the masked ball (another one on my bucket list!). The Scala Rio nightclub, Avenida Afrânio, also hosts 6 different balls (including a gay ball) during the carnival for dressing up and dancing yet again! I attended a carnival ball at the Monte Libano club in 2016 and was greatly disappointed by both the confused service at the entrance and the extortionate price (500 reais!) to find a seat upstairs. Better to confine yourself to a street party or carnival parade downtown in Avenida Rio Branco (free) or in Samba Land in Praça Onze at only 15 reais for entry. Samba Land in 2017 is open February 17-18th and February 24-27th, and March 2-3rd starting at 7pm until 6am.

Reminder to make sure you have travel insurance. Also, the UPA emergency hospital in the Copacabana is located in front of the Sigueira Campus Metro exit and is clean, efficient and open 24hr.

Chapter 12

A Few Useful Phrases

bom dia – good day
boa tarde – good afternoon
boa noite – good night
obrigado (a) – thank you
com licença – excuse me
tchau, adeus – goodbye
por favor – please
cardápio – menu
onde? – where?
banheiro – toilet
quanto? – how much?
desculpe – sorry
a conta, por favor – the bill please
preciso de ajuda por favor – I need help please

Chapter 13

Final Comment

Your visit to Brazil will be a wonderful experience and the above tips will just help you avoid annoying incidences so that you remain safe, healthy and within budget. Do, however, remember that you are a visitor and so do not expect things to function quite so quickly (especially the cashiers in the supermarkets!) as at home. Just relax, enjoy and be happy!

Lightning Source UK Ltd.
Milton Keynes UK
UKHW05f1523240818
327629UK00016B/108/P

9 781911 110002